# BIBLE 201: WHO
## CONTENTS

MW01121636

| | |
|---|---|
| **Author:** | **Patricia A. Goss, M.A.** |
| Editor: | Richard W. Wheeler, M.A.Ed. |
| Consulting Editor: | J. Howard Stitt, Th.M., Ed.D. |
| Revision Editor: | Alan Christopherson, M.S. |

# Alpha Omega Publications

300 North McKemy Avenue, Chandler, Arizona 85226-2618

ALPHA OMEGA
PUBLICATIONS

**Learn with the Bridgestone characters:**

 When you see me, I will help your teacher explain the exciting things you are expected to do.

 When you do actions with me, you will learn how to write, draw, match words, read, and much more.

 You and I will learn about matching words, listening, drawing, and other fun things in your lessons.

 Follow me and I will show you new, exciting truths, that will help you learn and understand what you study. Let's learn!

# WHO AM I?

My name is _____ .
Print your first and last name.

I know that God made me, _____ ,
Print first name.

the way He wanted me.

I know that I, _____ am **special**.
Print first name.

I know that God has a special plan for my life.
Now I want to do God's work.
I know that God will help me.
I know how God helped Daniel.

**Read these objectives.** They will tell you what you will be able to do when you have finished this LIFEPAC.

1. You will be able to tell how you are God's child.
2. You will be able to tell how God loves you.
3. You will be able to tell how you are special.
4. You will be able to name ways God shows love for you and helps you.
5. You will learn how to tell others about Jesus.
6. You will be able to recite four Bible verses.
7. You will be able to tell the story of Daniel.

# NEW WORDS

**begotten** (be got ten).  To be born of someone.

**deed.**  Something you do.

**everlasting** (ev er last ing).  Never ending.

**fearfully** (fear ful ly).  With great care and thought.

**heavenly** (heav en ly).  From heaven.

**Israelite** (Is ra el ite).  Someone from Israel.

**palace** (pal ace).  A king's home.

**perish** (per ish).  To pass away.  To die.

**praise.**  To give glory.  To honor.

**protect** (pro tect).  To take care of.  To bless.

**recite** (re cite).  To say from memory.

**ruler** (rul er).  Someone who is a leader, as a king.

**Saviour** (sav iour).  One who saves.  Jesus.

**sinful** (sin ful).  Full of sin.  Not obedient.

**special** (spe cial).  One who is set apart.

**vegetables** (veg e ta bles).  Plants that are food.

**whatsoever** (what so ev er).  All things.

**whosoever** (who so ev er).  Anyone.

**wonderfully** (won der ful ly).  Very good.

These words will appear in **boldface** (darker print) the first time they are used.

# I.  GOD MADE US

God loves me.
That is why I am **special**.
I am very, very special.
God has a special plan for my life.
I **praise** His name.  Praise the Lord.

## WORDS TO STUDY

| | | |
|---|---|---|
| **fearfully** | (fear ful ly). | With great care and thought. |
| **heavenly** | (heav en ly). | From heaven. |
| **praise** | (praise). | To give glory.  To honor. |
| **special** | (spe cial). | One who is set apart. |
| **wonderfully** | (won der ful ly). | Very good. |

Ask your teacher to say these words with you.

 Teacher Check _____
                           Initial          Date

## ME

   I look in the mirror.
What do I see?
Some people have brown eyes.
Some people have blue eyes or green eyes.
God gave me eyes.

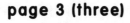

Some people have yellow hair.
Some people have brown hair
or red hair or black hair.
God gave me hair.

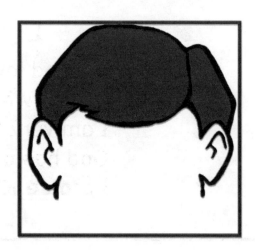

Some people are tall.
Some people are short.
Some people laugh a lot.
Some people are quiet.
Some people are quick.
Some people are slow.
God made me just the way
He wanted me.
God made me special.
No one else is like me.

(Paste a picture
of yourself
in this space.)

Print your first and last name.

**This picture is of me.**

God teaches us many lessons in the Bible.
The psalmist says in Psalm 139:14,
"I will praise Thee, for I am
**fearfully** and **wonderfully** made."
This verse tells that I have been made by God
in a very special way.

**Write what God has taught you.**

1.1    Who is fearfully and wonderfully made?

_____

1.2    Whom will I praise for making me?

_____

Thank God for making you special.
Bow your head and give thanks to God.

## MY FAMILY

Some people have a big family.
Some people have a small family.
God gave me my family.
God is my **heavenly** Father
and does all things by His plan.
In His plan, all things are done well.

**Draw a picture of your family.**

## My Family

 All people who believe in Jesus are in God's family.
**Write** yes **or** no **on the line.**

1.3     Do I believe in Jesus? _____

Jesus loves me so **very** much.
**Do this activity.**

1.4     Write the first four words of Psalm 139:14 on the lines.

_____

_____

## MY FRIENDS

Some people have many friends.
Some people have few friends.
I like to help my friends.

Helping my friends is fun.
God gives me friends.
Friends play with me.
Friends make me laugh when I am sad.
I like to make friends laugh when they are sad.
   Jesus wants to be my best Friend.
Jesus will be with me
when my friends have gone home.

---

**Write** yes **or** no **on the line.**

1.5   Is Jesus my best Friend? _____

1.6   Does God give me friends? _____

**Finish these sentences.**

1.7   My best Friend is _____ .

1.8   Psalm 139:14 "I will praise Thee; _____

_____ . "

---

## MY LIFE

   God knows me better than anyone else.
God made me.
God has a special plan for my life.
He teaches me how to live.
He teaches me by His Word, the Bible.
God's way is the best way.

**Dot-to-dot.** Begin with 1. Your picture will show God's way.

1.9

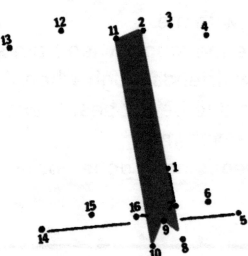

The B ___ bl ___

**Write the missing letters on the lines.**

1.10    The B _____ bl _____

**Circle the right word.** Write the word on the line.

1.11    God has a _____ plan for my life.

　　　　　　good　　　　　funny　　　　　special

1.12    _____ knows me better than anyone else.

　　　　　Mother　　　　　God　　　　　Father

**Write the missing words on the lines.**

1.13    Psalm 139:14 "I will _____ Thee; for I am

　　　　fearfully and _____ made."

- - - - - - - - - - - - - - - - - - - - - - - - - - - - - - - - - - - -

For this Self Test, study what you have read and done.
The Self Test will check what you remember.

# SELF TEST 1

**Draw a line to the right word.**

1.01  Some people have red                me

1.02  Some people are                     family

1.03  Some people have a big              hair

1.04  God made me                         slow

1.05  No one is just like                 special

**Write the missing words.**

1.06  Psalm 139:14 " _____ _____ praise Thee; for _____ _____ fearfully and wonderfully _____ ."

**Circle Yes or No.**

1.07  God does all things well.                               Yes        No

1.08  The Bible shows me God's way.                           Yes        No

1.09  My teacher knows me better than anyone else.           Yes        No

1.010  Jesus loves me very much.                             Yes        No

1.011  All people who believe in Jesus are in God's family.  Yes        No

**Circle the right word.**  Write the word on the line.

1.012  _____ wants to be your best friend.

   Everybody        She            He            Jesus

1.013  God has a _____ plan for your life.

   special            big              pretty

1.014 _____ way is the best way.

     My               God's            Any

1.015 Everyone who believes in Jesus is in God's _____ .

     room            town          family

1.016 God is my _____ Father and does all things well.

     Sunday         heavenly        big

$\frac{16}{20}$ Teacher Check _____

                         Initial        Date

                                          My Score

## II. GOD LOVES ME

My name is _____ .

                  Print your first and last name.

I am so happy.
I am happy that God made me.
I am happy because I will learn why God loves me.
God will teach me many things.
He will teach me the good things in life.

---

**WORDS TO STUDY**

| | | |
|---|---|---|
| **begotten** | (be got ten) | To be born of someone. |
| **everlasting** | (ev er last ing) | Never ending. |
| **perish** | (per ish) | To pass away.  To die. |
| **Saviour** | (sav iour) | One who saves.  Jesus. |
| **sinful** | (sin ful) | Full of sin.  Not obedient. |
| **whosoever** | (who so ev er) | Anyone. |

---

Ask your teacher to say these words with you.

Teacher Check _____

                  Initial       Date

## GOD GAVE HIS SON, JESUS

God made me
and wants me to be His child.
God is good.
He knows what I need.
I am not always obedient.
I do not always
do the right thing.

God wants me to know
what He is like.
He sent His Son, Jesus.
Jesus came to save me.
In the Bible God says,

"For God so loved the world that He
gave His only **begotten** Son, that
**whosoever** believeth in Him should not
**perish**, but have **everlasting** life."

(John 3:16)

God tells me that I may live
with Him always if I believe:
1. that Jesus is God's Son,
2. that I need to be saved, and
3. that Jesus died to save me.

Someday my body may die,
but I will still live in Heaven,
because I believe in Jesus.

God will give me a new body.
I will never be sick.
I will never be bad.
I will never be sad.

Each day we should thank God
for sending Jesus to us.
Thank you, God.
Thank you for sending Jesus.

**Thank you, God!**

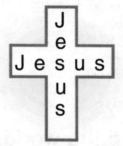

---

 **Write what God has taught you.**

2.1    Circle the words that tell something about God.

loves me              does not care              sent Jesus

2.2    Circle the words that tell you something about you.
You . . .

are always good.    need Jesus.        can feel sad.

2.3    Write a sentence telling why God sent Jesus.

_____ .

2.4    These words tell about Jesus. Make a dot **under** the
short vowels. Draw a line **over** the long vowels.

sent        helps        God          live          Bible

best        Him          saves us    gave          knows

Jesus came to teach me.
I am saved by Jesus
if I believe in Him.
The way Jesus lived
teaches me how to live.
Jesus told many stories
in the Bible.
These stories teach me how to live.

Jesus said that
the best way to live is
to love one another.
I am happy that Jesus came to teach me.

**Jesus came to teach
us how to live.**

---

**Write the missing letters on the lines.**

2.5     Jesus teaches me by the way He l ___ v ___ d.

2.6     Jesus teaches me by His st ___ r ___ ___ s.

2.7     Jesus teaches me by what He s ___ ___ d.

2.8     Jesus came to t ___ ___ ch me and to s ___ v ___ me.

Teacher Check _____
                Initial         Date

---

Jesus came to SAVE me and to TEACH me.
Jesus came to HELP me, too.
When I need help,
I can ask Jesus.
He knows me and wants
to help me.

I can talk to Him.
I can read my Bible
to know what Jesus says.
Jesus loves me.

 **Read each sentence and do what each tells you to do.**

2.9     Circle the words that tell why Jesus came to us.

lost        save        help        teach        feel        stop

2.10    Write the words that have short vowels on the lines below.

_____        _____        _____

2.11    Write the three words that tell why Jesus came.

_____        _____        _____

2.12    Make a face in the circle to show how you feel right now.

**Write the correct name on each line.**

Jesus          God

2.13    Who sent Jesus?                    _____

2.14    Who came to teach me?          _____

2.15    I am God's child
        because of                          _____

2.16    Who came to save me?           _____

**Write the correct word on each line.**

life            whosoever            perish

2.17    "For God so loved the world that He gave His only

        begotten Son, that _____ believeth

        in Him should not _____ , but have

        everlasting _____ ." (John 3:16)

# I CAN BELIEVE IN JESUS

The Bible tells me
that all people are sinful.
When I want to be obedient,
I need God's help.
I am sinful.

**I need God's help.**

My sin makes God sad.
God knows my sin hurts me.
God wants me to be happy.
God wants me to live forever.

Jesus said,
"I am the Way, the Truth, and the Life,
no man cometh unto the Father, but by me."

The only way I can know God, the Father,
is by believing in Jesus as my Lord and **Saviour**.

## GOD GAVE HIS WORD, THE BIBLE

God wants me to know Him.
He is my heavenly Father.
God gave us His Word, the Bible.
The Bible teaches me about God.
He told some special people
what to write in the Bible.
They did not write their own words.
The people wrote
what God told them to write.
It took many years for all of
the Bible to be written.
I have the Bible.
I praise the Lord for the Bible.
I know how to believe in Jesus.
I can know God.
God talks to me in the Bible.

**It took many years
to write the Bible.**

**God talks to me in
the Bible.**

**Try this puzzle.**

2.18    Write the missing words in the puzzle.

LOVE    PEOPLE    GOD    BIBLE    JESUS    FOREVER

| ACROSS | DOWN |
|---|---|
| 4.    Who is my heavenly Father? | 1.    What is God's Word? |
| 5.    What does Jesus tell me to do? | 2.    Who did God tell to write the Bible? |
| 6.    Who is my Lord and Saviour? | 3.    How long will I live if I believe in Jesus? |

For this Self Test, study what you have read and done. The Self Test will check what you remember.

## SELF TEST 2

**Write the missing words on the lines.**

2.01    "For _____ so loved the world, that He _____ His only begotten _____ that whosoever believeth in _____ should not perish, but have everlasting _____."
(John 3:16)

**Circle Yes or No.**

| | | | |
|---|---|---|---|
| 2.02 | God made me special. | Yes | No |
| 2.03 | It took one year for the Bible to be written. | Yes | No |
| 2.04 | I need God's help. | Yes | No |
| 2.05 | God talks to me in the Bible. | Yes | No |
| 2.06 | I am wonderfully and fearfully made. | Yes | No |
| 2.07 | All people sin. | Yes | No |
| 2.08 | Jesus came to save me. | Yes | No |
| 2.09 | Jesus died to save me. | Yes | No |
| 2.010 | Sad people live in Heaven. | Yes | No |
| 2.011 | Jesus is the Way, the Truth, and the Life. | Yes | No |

## Draw a line to the correct word.

2.012    Who is my heavenly Father?          Jesus

2.013    Who is my Lord and Saviour?      Bible

2.014    What is God's Word?            love

2.015    Who did God tell to write
the Bible?                            forever

2.016    What does Jesus tell me to do?   people

2.017    How long will I live if Jesus
is my Saviour?                   God

## Write three words that tell why God gave His Son, Jesus.

2.018    to _____ me       to _____ me

          to _____ me

## Write two words telling who Jesus is.

2.019    Jesus is my _____ .

          Jesus is my _____ .

# III. GOD HELPS ME

God helps me in my work.
He helps me when I am sad.
God helps me tell others
about Jesus.

**God helps me help others.**

## WORDS TO STUDY

| | | |
|---|---|---|
| **deed** | | Something you do. |
| **recite** | (re cite) | To say from memory. |
| **whatsoever** | (what so ev er) | All things. |

Ask your teacher to say these words with you.

 Teacher Check _____

               Initial            Date

## IN MY WORK

I am God's child.
I have special work to do.
Doing this work will make God
very happy. Pleasing God
means to make Him very happy.
When I please God that makes
me happy, too. God will show
me what to do. If I don't obey
Him, God will not be pleased.

**God helps me to be
happy in my work.**

**Do these activities.** Write your answer.

3.1    Write a sentence telling why you should work for God.

_____

_____ .


3.2    How do you feel inside when you do something nice for someone?

_____

_____ .


God teaches us in Colossians 3:17,
"**Whatsoever** ye do in word or **deed**,
do all in the name of the Lord Jesus,
giving thanks to God . . ."
Can you **recite** this verse
from the Word of God?


Do I do good deeds so people will think
that I am good?
No!  Because God helps me, I can do good deeds.
When I do good works,
people will know that Jesus is good.
Now that Jesus is living in me,
He helps me do good work.
I can't do it by myself.

**Circle the word in each sentence that tells how I can work for God in Jesus' name.**

3.3    Be helpful to others.

3.4    Be kind to others.

3.5    Be honest to others.

3.6    Obey my father and my mother.

3.7    Be loving to others.

**Choose the correct word from the words you just circled.** Write the word on the line.

3.8    What word sounds like find? _____

3.9    What word sounds like day? _____

**Look at the picture.**

Do you know how to be helpful?
Is someone being helpful
in the picture?

These words go together.
See if you can read all of them.

| | | |
|---|---|---|
| hang up clothes | love others | fill up tub |
| use nice words | empty trash | pick up toys |
| look after baby | | |

# BIBLE

## 2 0 1

## LIFEPAC TEST

29 / 36

Name _____

Date _____

Score _____

# BIBLE 201: LIFEPAC TEST

**Circle the right word.**

1. Someone who leads.

    Israelite          ruler                begotten

2. To say from memory.

    praise             perish               recite

3. Never ending.

    heavenly           everlasting          sinful

4. To take care of.

    fearfully          whatsoever           protect

5. Saviour.

    Darius             Jesus                Nebuchadnezzar

**Write the missing words on the lines.**

6. "For _____ so _____ the world that _____ gave His only begotten _____ , that whosoever believeth in _____ should not perish but _____ everlasting _____."

    (John 3:16)

**Circle Yes or No.**

7. The only way I can know God the Father is by believing in Jesus as my Saviour.

    Yes                No

8. God says that I am to do good works so people will know Jesus is good.

Yes               No

9. Daniel and his friends could not eat the vegetables.

Yes               No

10. I am God's child only when I do good.

Yes               No

11. I should tell others about believing in Jesus.

Yes               No

## Write the missing words on the lines.

12. " _____ _____ praise Thee; for _____ _____ fearfully and wonderfully _____ . . ." (Psalm 139:14)

## Write Yes or No.

13. God tells me that I may live with Him forever if I:

_____ a. Believe that Jesus is His Son.

_____ b. Believe that I need to be saved.

_____ c. Believe that Jesus died to save me.

## Write the missing words on the lines.

12. "And whatsoever _____ do in _____ or deed, do _____ in the _____ of the Lord _____ , giving thanks to God. . ." (Colossians 3:17)

## Write a sentence telling why God sent Jesus.

15. _____

    _____

## Write the missing words on the lines.

16. "_____ answered and said, 'Blessed be

    the _____ of _____ for ever and

    _____ : for wisdom and might are

    _____ .'" (Daniel 2:20)

# NOTES

**Write the words from the box that go together**.
The first one is done for you.

h <u>ang up clothes</u>

3.10     e _____

3.11     l _____

3.12     p _____

3.13     f _____

3.14     u _____

3.15     l _____

Read the first letter of each row above.
If you will read down the row,
you will see that the letters spell a word.
What is that word?

3.16     The word is _____ .

You have just written ways you can be helpful.
Can you think of others?

## IN MY FEELINGS

Sometimes I feel sad.
Sometimes I am angry.
Sometimes I am tired.
Sometimes I don't understand
things.

**Sometimes I feel sad.**

God helps me in these times.

He knows me.

God can tell me what to do if I ask Him.

When I need help,

I can read my Bible.

God can show me what to do.

If I cannot read my Bible,

I can pray to God.

He will talk to me

if I listen to Him.

He will help me think of what to do.

I will always thank God.

I will always thank Him

for helping me.

**Circle the right word.** Write it on the line.

3.17    God _____ help me when I feel angry.

    a.    can                         b.    cannot

3.18    I _____ ask Him for help.

    a.    must                      b.    must not

3.19    The Bible _____ tell me God's words to help me.

    a.    will                       b.    will not

3.20    I _____ pray to God.

    a.    should                  b.    should not

3.21    I _____ always thank Him.

    a.    must                      b.    must not

**Read Colossians 3:17 in your Bible.** Ask your teacher to read the verse with you. Try to recite the verse to your teacher.

Teacher Check _____

Initial                        Date

## IN MY SPECIAL WORK FOR HIM

God has special work for me to do.
Our world has many people.
People are everywhere.
Many people do not know about God's love.

God loves us.  He gave His Son, Jesus,
to die for us.

We want to talk to people about
the love of God.
Sometimes we can even show
the love of Jesus.
How do you show the love of Jesus?

We can love others as we like to be loved.
We can be kind to others
as we would like others to be kind to us.
We can show the love of Jesus
by what we do and what we say.

This little saying teaches us this truth.

It's not what you say.
It's not what you think.
It's not what you write in pen and ink.
It's what you do that's you!

Yes, what you do is the real you.
When you are kind,
that's you.
When you love others,
that's you.
That is the love of Jesus in you.

 **Write a sentence telling what special work God gave you.**

3.22 _____

_____

The Bible tells me
that everyone has sinned.
When we sin, we are not close to God.
We are lost.
God has helped us
by giving His Son, Jesus, to save us.

Jesus takes our sin out of God's sight.
Then we can be close to God in Heaven.

I want my friends and loved ones
to be close to God, too.
I want them to love God like I do.

I can tell my friends how God wants us to let Him love us.

1.  Everyone has sinned and is lost.
2.  God loves you and gave His Son Jesus to die for
    your sin.
3.  You need to believe in Jesus as your Saviour.
4.  God will forgive you and save you from sin.
5.  You will have everlasting life.
6.  Tell others that Jesus is your Saviour.

**Draw a line to the right word.**

3.23   Who has sinned?                     Jesus

3.24   What will God do?                    God

3.25   Who will be your Saviour?           everyone

3.26   Who do you tell you are sorry?      forgive

Teacher Check _____
                    Initial              Date

**page 27 (twenty-seven)**

For this Self Test, study what you have read and done. The Self Test will check what you remember.

## SELF TEST 3

**Write the missing words on the lines.**

3.01 "And whatsoever _____ do in _____ or
_____ , do all in the name of the Lord
_____ , giving _____ to God. . . "
(Colossians 3:17)

**Circle the right word.**

3.02 To be born of someone.
everlasting          perish          begotten

3.03 To do what God wants.
love          sin          forget

3.04 To say from memory.
recite          praise          fearfully

3.05 Not doing what God wants.
love          sin          forget

3.06 To honor.
heavenly          praise          recite

**Circle Yes or No.**

3.07 I should thank God.                                Yes          No

3.08 Doing God's work makes me happy.  Yes          No

3.09 God helps me when I am sad.            Yes          No

3.010 Jesus helps me love others.             Yes          No

3.011 I should do all things in the
name of Jesus.                                      Yes          No

**Read these words.** Write nine of these words on the lines in the sentences. One word is an extra word. You will not need it.

ask　　　　believe　　　forgive　　　kind　　　　help
love　　　　loving　　　　teach　　　　save　　　　honest

## Write the missing words.

3.012　　God sent Jesus to _____, _____, and
　　　　_____ me

3.013　　I can work for God by being _____, _____,
　　　　and _____ .

3.014　　Jesus can help me _____ others.

3.015　　God will show you what to do if you _____
　　　　God for help.

3.016　　If you tell God you are sorry, He will _____
　　　　you.

Teacher Check _____
　　　　　　　Initial　　　　Date

My Score

20/24

# IV. GOD HELPED DANIEL

This wonderful story is
about a young boy named Daniel.
The story of Daniel is one
of the greatest stories in the Bible.

Daniel learned to trust in God.
God helped Daniel
in a wonderful way.

## WORDS TO STUDY

| | | |
|---|---|---|
| **Israelite** | (Is ra el ite) | Someone from Israel. |
| **palace** | (pal ace) | A king's home. |
| **protect** | (pro tect) | To take care of. |
| **ruler** | (rul er) | Someone who leads. |
| **vegetables** | (veg e ta bles) | Plants that are food. |

Ask your teacher to say these words with you.

 Teacher Check _____
                          Initial                    Date

## DANIEL LOVED GOD

The Bible tells about a boy named Daniel.
He lived in Israel.
People who lived in Israel
were called **Israelites**.

Daniel loved God very much.
Daniel talked to God every day.
Daniel read God's Word to learn
about how God wanted him to live.

Daniel was a strong boy.
Daniel was a smart boy.

**Daniel was a strong
and a smart boy.**

**Draw a line to the right word. Write the word on
the line.** The first one is done for you.

|     | Daniel loved | God | . | smart |
| --- | --- | --- | --- | --- |
| 4.1 | Daniel read | | . | God |
| 4.2 | Daniel lived in | | . | God's Word |
| 4.3 | Daniel's body was | | . | strong |
| 4.4 | Daniel was very | | . | Israel |

A king named Nebuchadnezzar
(Neb u chad nez zer) was a **ruler**
in the country of Babylon (Bab y lon).
He wanted to rule the Israelites, too.
He sent men to burn down
the Israelites' homes.

Then he took the Israelites
to his country of Babylon.
He made the Israelites
work very hard for him.

King Nebuchadnezzar wanted
the strong and smart boys
to live in his **palace**.
Daniel was taken from his family.
The king wanted Daniel
to live in his palace.
So Daniel had to live in the king's palace.

**Can you find the way Daniel went to the palace?**

4.5

**Draw a line under all the short vowels in the King's name.**

4.6    K I N G    N E B U C H A D N E Z Z A R

Can you say the king's name?
Read the king's name to your teacher.

## DANIEL OBEYED GOD

   The palace was very big.
Daniel missed his family.
Daniel was not lonely, because
Daniel talked to God every day.
Daniel wanted to live God's way.
God had a special plan for Daniel's life.
Daniel trusted God.

   The king wanted the Israelite boys
to eat his rich food.
Daniel wanted to obey God's Word.
He did not want to eat the king's food.

**The Israelite boys did not want to eat the king's rich food.**

Daniel and three friends said,
"No, we would like to have water
and **vegetables**, please."

For ten days the four boys ate vegetables
and drank water.
All the other boys ate the king's food.
After ten days Daniel and his three friends
looked very strong.
The boys eating the king's food
were not as strong.

From then on,
the four boys ate only vegetables
and drank water.
God took good care of them.
They wanted to obey God's Word.

**Do you know the answer?**

4.7    WHO wanted to obey God's Word? _____

_____

4.8    WHERE were the Israelite boys taken? _____

4.9    WHY did Daniel not want to eat the king's food?

_____

4.10    WHEN did Daniel and his friends look very strong?

_____

## GOD BLESSED DANIEL

Daniel and his three friends
obeyed God's rules about food.
God made Daniel and his three friends
able to learn and to be very smart.

God gave Daniel a special gift.
This gift was to let Daniel know
the meaning of dreams.

**Do these activities**.

4.11    Circle the words that tell how God blessed Daniel.

able to learn        be very smart        live in a palace
know the meaning of dreams

4.12    Circle the words that tell how God blesses you.
gave me a family
gave me friends
gave me a healthy body
made me able to learn
gave me a happy heart
gave me a good school

4.13    Bow your head and thank God for all His blessings
upon you.

God gives me what I need.
God knew what Daniel would need, too.
King Nebuchadnezzar had a bad dream.
He could not remember the dream.

He was afraid.
He wanted to know about the dream.

All of the king's wise men
could not help him.
They could not tell the king about his dream.
The king was very angry.
He was going to kill all the wise men.

Daniel did not want the men to be killed.
Daniel asked God to tell him the meaning
of the king's dream.

That night,
God told Daniel about the king's dream.
Only God could know about the dream.

Daniel was so happy.
The Bible tells us that Daniel answered and said,

" . . .Blessed (wonderful)
be the name of God
for ever and ever:
for wisdom (to know everything)
and might (to be strong) are His."
(Daniel 2:20)

The next day,
Daniel told the king
what God had said about the dream.
The king was so thankful
he fell down at Daniel's feet.

King Nebuchadnezzar said,
"Your God is the only true God."

The king gave Daniel many great gifts.
The king made Daniel a great ruler
over all the wise men.

 **Read Daniel 2:20 in your Bible.** Write the answer on the line.

4.14　Who was Daniel talking to? _____

4.15　What did Daniel call the name of God? _____

_____

4.16　How long will God's name be called Blessed? _____

_____

4.17　What does God have? _____

 **Use the Bible.**

4.18　The verse Daniel 2:20 helps me to tell how wonderful God is.  I will find a friend and say Daniel 2:20 to my friend.

 **Tell a picture story.**

4.19　Look at the four pictures on the next page.  Which picture happened first?  Write the number on the line below the picture.

Which picture happened second?  Which one happened third?  Which happened fourth?

# Daniel and the King

King asking wise men
to tell him his dream

_____

King falling down
on knees in thanks
to Daniel and his God

_____

The king sleeping
and having a dream.

_____

Daniel asks God
to tell him the
king's dream.

_____

**Match these words.** Draw a line from the word in Row **A** to the word in Row **B** that sounds the same.

4.20

|  A  |  B  |
|-----|-----|
| told | well |
| fight | might |
| king | ring |
| fell | fold |
| mad | cream |
| dream | dad |

## GOD PROTECTED DANIEL

God had blessed Daniel so much.
Some people did not like Daniel
because he had so many blessings.

A new king named Darius (Dar  i  us)
made Daniel a great ruler.
He made Daniel a ruler
over all the people.
Some leaders wanted to have Daniel killed.
The leaders tricked the king
into making a new law.
The law said that
everyone must pray only to the king
for the next 30 days.
If they prayed to anyone else,
they would be put into the lions' den.

Daniel knew about the law.
But Daniel would pray only to God
as he always had.
To know that God will **protect** you
is to have faith.
Daniel had faith.

**God protected Daniel**

The leaders told King Darius
about Daniel praying to God.
King Darius was sorry he had made this law.
The king did not want Daniel killed.
The leaders said that Daniel must be put into the
lions' den.
Daniel was put into the den of hungry lions.
King Darius was so sad that
he could not sleep.

Daniel knew that God would protect him.

God did not let the lions hurt Daniel.

The next morning
the king went to the lions' den.
He called to Daniel,
"Has your God been able to save you?"

King Darius was very surprised
when Daniel said,
"Yes, my God
has shut the mouths of the lions."

The king was very happy.
The king said to Daniel,
"Your God is the only true God."

Daniel had a happy life
being a ruler for King Darius.
Daniel obeyed God.
Daniel was blessed by God.
Daniel was protected by God.

 **Write the missing word on each line.**

4.21   The leaders did not like Daniel because he was

_____.

bad                      big                      blessed

4.22   The leaders _____ the king into making a
new law.

talked                   tricked                  praised

4.23   Daniel _____ the new law.

knew about            liked                    obeyed

4.24   King Darius was _____ he had made the law.

glad                     sorry                    thankful

**Write the missing word on each line.**

4.25  Daniel had _____ that God would protect him.

faith                    dreams                    wished

4.26  The king said that Daniel's God was the only _____
God.

happy                    smart                    true

**Write the missing letters.**

4.27  Daniel ob __ __ __ d God.

4.28  God b __ __ s __ __ d Daniel.

4.29  God pr __ t __ c __ __ d Daniel.

4.30  If I o __ __ __ God, He will b __ __ __ __ me
and p __ __ __ __ __ __ me.

**Draw a straight line over each long vowel.  Draw a
(/) mark over each silent e.**

| 4.31 | leaders | 4.34 | protect | 4.37 | name |
| 4.32 | rule | 4.35 | read | 4.38 | write |
| 4.33 | like | 4.36 | make | | |

**Now, write the five words that have the silent
final e.**

4.39  _____          4.42  _____

4.40  _____          4.43  _____

4.41  _____

Study what you have read and done for this last Self Test. This Self Test will check what you remember in your studies of all parts of the LIFEPAC. The last Self Test will tell you what parts of the LIFEPAC you need to study again.

## SELF TEST 4

**Write the missing words on the lines.**

might     God     Blessed     wisdom     Daniel

4.01    "Daniel answered and said, " _____
be the name of _____ for ever and ever: for
_____ , and _____ , are His"
(Daniel 2:20).

**Circle Yes or No.**

4.02    God has a special plan for my life.
Yes                          No

4.03    God had a special plan for Daniel's life.
Yes                          No

4.04    God says that I may live forever with Him if I believe in His Son.
Yes                          No

4.05    Jesus is my Saviour if I believe in Him.
Yes                          No

4.06    I do good work so that people will think I am good.
Yes                          No

**Draw a line to the correct word.**

| | | |
|---|---|---|
| 4.07 | God sent His only begotten | made |
| 4.08 | Daniel was an | child |
| 4.09 | I am God's | Bible |
| 4.010 | God teaches me in the | blessed |
| 4.011 | Daniel called God | Israelite |
| 4.012 | All people have | Son |
| 4.013 | Jesus commands me to | Jesus |
| 4.014 | My Lord and Saviour is | sinned |
| 4.015 | My heavenly Father is | love |
| 4.016 | I am fearfully and wonderfully | God |

**Write the missing word on the line.**

4.017    Daniel trusted God to _____ him.
      thank              protect           praise

4.018    God _____ Daniel to know the meaning of dreams.
      **asked**           **blessed**           **did not want**

4.019    The leaders wanted to _____ Daniel.
      kill              like           surprise

4.020    King Darius was _____ to find Daniel safe.
      **sad**           **angry**           **happy**

4.021    King Darius said that Daniel's God was the _____ God.
      true              best           smart

# Circle the words that tell how God blessed Daniel.

4.022    a great ruler       a strong body       to kill lions

                  understand dreams      to be very smart

$\dfrac{22}{28}$    Teacher Check _____

                            Initial             Date

My Score

---

Before taking the LIFEPAC Test, you should do these self checks.

1. _____ Did you do good work on your last Self Test?

2. _____ Did you study again those parts of the LIFEPAC you didn't remember?

                    Check one:  ☐  Yes  (good)

                                ☐  No  (ask your teacher)

3. _____ Do you know all the new words in "Words to Study"?

                    Check one:  ☐  Yes  (good)

                                ☐  No  (ask your teacher)

# NOTES